FRACKING

CHERITON
CHILDREN'S BOOKS

Please visit our website, www.cheritonchildrensbooks.com to see more of our high-quality books.

First Edition

Published in 2022 by **Cheriton Children's Books**
PO Box 7258, Bridgnorth WV16 9ET, UK

© 2022 Cheriton Children's Books

Author: Robyn Hardyman
Designer: Paul Myerscough
Editor: Victoria Garrard
Proofreader: Wendy Scavuzzo
Picture Researcher: Rachel Blount
Consultant: David Hawksett, BSc

Picture credits: Cover: Shutterstock/Calin Tatu; Inside: p1: Shutterstock/Nightman1965; p3: Shutterstock/Trabantos; p4: Shutterstock/Viktoriia Hnatiuk; p5: Shutterstock/ Sarah2; p6: Shutterstock/ VectorMine; p7: Shutterstock/FerrezFrames; p8: Shutterstock/ Tlindsayg; p9: Shutterstock/Everett Historical; p11t: Shutterstock/A Katz; p11b: Shutterstock/ Corlaffra; p12: Shutterstock/Harry Beugelink; p13: Shutterstock/Alexander Oganezov; p14: Shutterstock/Stephenallen75; p15: Shutterstock/Billion Photos: p16; Shutterstock/Inked Pixels; p17: Shutterstock/Alizada Studios; p18: Shutterstock/ LanaElcova; p19t: Shutterstock/Porcupen/Paul Myerscough; p19b: Shutterstock/ Dewald Kirsten; p20: Shutterstock/Bruce Goerlitz Photo; p21: Shutterstock/ PaigeWhite; p22: Shutterstock/Jim Parkin; p23: Shutterstock/FerrezFrames; p24: Shutterstock/Trabantos; p25: Shutterstock/Nightman1965; p26: Shutterstock/Randi Sokoloff; p27: Shutterstock/ Seeshooteatrepeat; p28: Shutterstock/AL PARKER PHOTOGRAPHY; p29: Shutterstock/ Philip Schubert; p30: Wikimedia Commons/ Joshua Doubek; p31: Shutterstock/ FerrezFrames; p32: Shutterstock/NeonLight; p33: Shutterstock/FerrezFrames; p34: Wikimedia Commons/Joshua Doubek; p35: Shutterstock/Anton Mackey; p36-37: Shutterstock/Pik56; p38: Shutterstock/Christopher Halloran; p39: Shutterstock/ Pictureguy; p40: Flickr/U.S. Department of Energy; p41: Shutterstock/Kris Wiktor; p42: Shutterstock/Allensima; p43: Shutterstock/Rena Schild; p44: Shutterstock/SFIO CRACHO; p45: Shutterstock/ Vaclav Volrab.

Printed in the United States of America

Contents

CHAPTER 1

What Is Fracking?

The world today faces the huge challenge of how to meet its ever-increasing need for energy. The global population is growing, and we are using more and more energy to power our homes, businesses, and transportation systems. The energy industry is working hard to develop new ways to provide this energy. One of the methods it is exploring is fracking.

Using Up Fossil Fuels

More than half of the energy the world uses comes from burning coal, oil, and natural gas in **power plants**. Coal, oil, and natural gas are **fossil fuels** that took millions of years to form underground. They are in limited supply, so they are called **nonrenewable** energy sources.

We burn fossil fuels when we travel—whether by car, bus, train, or airplane. We need to find alternatives to fossil fuels before we run out of our supplies.

Getting to the Gas

Traditionally, natural gas has been extracted by drilling deep holes into the natural **reservoirs** of gas underground. The weight of all the rock above squeezes and pressurizes the gas. Because it is under pressure, drilling into it allows it to escape upward to the surface. It's a little like making a hole in a plastic bottle, then squeezing it—water only comes out when pressure is applied. However, not all gas is found in reservoirs. There is a lot of gas trapped inside a type of rock called shale.

If you drill into shale, the gas does not flow out to the surface, so experts have had to find a way to extract it. "Fracking" is short for hydraulic fracturing, which is the process used to extract the gas. The process involves injecting liquid at high pressure into the shale rock. This opens up the cracks in the shale so the gas can escape. The gas then flows through a pipe to a **wellhead** at the surface.

A Fracking Boom

In the last decade, there has been a fracking boom in the United States. The number of natural gas **wells** has more than doubled. This has produced a lot more gas at affordable prices, and means the country has had to import, or bring in, less fuel from other countries.

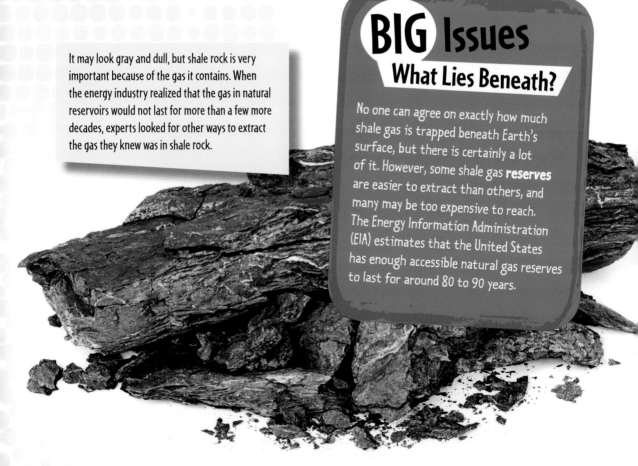

It may look gray and dull, but shale rock is very important because of the gas it contains. When the energy industry realized that the gas in natural reservoirs would not last for more than a few more decades, experts looked for other ways to extract the gas they knew was in shale rock.

BIG Issues
What Lies Beneath?

No one can agree on exactly how much shale gas is trapped beneath Earth's surface, but there is certainly a lot of it. However, some shale gas **reserves** are easier to extract than others, and many may be too expensive to reach. The Energy Information Administration (EIA) estimates that the United States has enough accessible natural gas reserves to last for around 80 to 90 years.

How Does It Work?

The process of fracking for shale gas is quite new. In 1990, engineers figured out how to drill vertically into rock, then bend the drill, so it drilled horizontally through a layer of shale rock. As a result, the fracking industry quickly grew, and huge amounts of shale gas became available for extraction around the world.

Down and Along

During the fracking process, the vertical well is drilled to a depth of 1 to 2 miles (1.6 to 3.2 km) until it reaches the level of the shale. The well is encased, or covered, in steel or cement to make it strong and to prevent any gas leaking into the surrounding ground. Once the well has reached the desired depth, the drill turns and starts to drill horizontally through the shale.

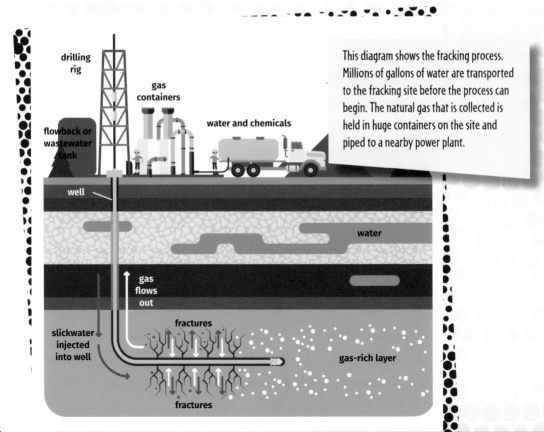

drilling rig

gas containers

water and chemicals

flowback or wastewater tank

well

water

gas flows out

slickwater injected into well

fractures

gas-rich layer

fractures

This diagram shows the fracking process. Millions of gallons of water are transported to the fracking site before the process can begin. The natural gas that is collected is held in huge containers on the site and piped to a nearby power plant.

Under Pressure

The next step in the fracking process is to pump fluid into the well at a very high pressure. This pressure is high enough to fracture, or crack, the surrounding rock, creating a lot of tiny cracks through which the gas can flow. The pumped fluid is called slickwater. Slickwater is water mixed with chemicals, with added sand and **ceramic particles**. The chemicals kill **bacteria** that might block the well, and **dissolve minerals** in the rock. Once the sand and ceramic particles are inside the shale, they prop open the cracks that were made in it. A lot of water is used in fracking—5 million gallons (19 million l) or more for each shale gas well, which is the amount contained in at least eight Olympic-sized swimming pools.

The flowback collects in huge tanks at the surface, before it is pumped back underground or sent elsewhere to be treated and cleaned.

Collecting the Gas

Next, the shale gas begins to flow out of the fracked rock into special tubes that are inserted into the well. These take the gas to the surface. Pipelines then carry the gas to a power plant, where it is burned to create electricity. The fluid used in the fracking process is now called flowback, or wastewater, and it is returned to the surface. It is taken to huge settling ponds or tanks on the fracking site. The flowback is very salty and contains harmful substances such as metals and the **radioactive** gas, radon. This collected fluid is then either pumped back deep underground or taken to wastewater treatment plants. Dealing with such huge amounts of wastewater is very expensive and complex. Small-scale water treatment plants often struggle to process it properly due to the huge amounts of flowback involved.

How Can Fracking Help Us?

Fracking has changed the energy industry in the United States. It has provided a huge amount of natural gas, which has reduced prices for everyone, from business owners to household users. It has also meant that we don't need to import as much gas from other countries.

Cleaning Up

Using fossil fuels is not a clean way to create electricity. Extracting coal from the ground produces twice as much **carbon dioxide** as fracking for shale gas produces, and carbon dioxide is a harmful gas that is causing great damage to the planet. The gas builds up in the **atmosphere**, trapping more heat from the sun than is natural.

This leads to **global warming**, a gradual process that is having an impact on the **climate** and weather of the whole planet. Extracting and burning coal also releases other harmful substances into the atmosphere. We must urgently reduce the amount of coal we burn in power plants if we are to slow global warming and stop the damage we are causing to the planet.

Power plants that burn coal to produce electricity, like this one, spew carbon dioxide and other gases into the atmosphere, contributing to global warming and **climate change**.

BIG Issues
An Unstable World

Fossil fuels are not evenly distributed across the world. For example, many countries in the Middle East have large underground supplies of oil. Their **economies** depend on exporting the oil, or selling it to other countries around the world. When these countries have **political** difficulties or are at war, their ability to supply oil or gas becomes unreliable. They may also decide to withhold or limit the supply to make it more expensive. Countries that are not rich in fossil fuels are tackling this problem by making themselves more energy self-sufficient. They are trying to create their own energy from sources such the wind or the sun. By doing so, they are becoming less reliant on the fossil-fuel rich countries they have depended on in the past.

Plenty for Everyone

Global shale gas **resources** are enormous. Scientists think they could increase the world's total reserves of natural gas by almost half. Thanks to its extraction of shale gas, the United States now has much greater energy security, or safety. Its energy supply is safer because it comes from within the country. There is no need to depend on a supply from other parts of the world, where political or economic issues may make the supply of coal, oil, or natural gas unreliable or unaffordable. Supporters of fracking say that it has the potential to provide the same energy security in many other countries worldwide.

These oil fields in Kuwait were set on fire by soldiers from Iraq when they invaded the country in 1991. This made Kuwait's ability to supply oil to the world unreliable.

CHAPTER 2

Fracking: For or Against?

Fracking may unlock huge reserves of natural gas, but not everyone is for it. Some people say the process is unsafe and that it is causing great damage to the environment**. Other critics of fracking argue that we should not be concentrating on new ways of extracting fossil fuels at all, but on developing alternative sources of energy that are both** renewable **and clean.**

A Worldwide Problem

The development of fracking in the United States may have made the country use more natural gas and less coal to create electricity in its power plants, but what effect has it had on other countries? The problem is that the United States has not stopped mining the coal that causes **pollution** when it is burned. Instead, it simply exports this coal overseas to Asia, Europe, and the rest of the world for countries there to use in their power plants. In European countries such as Germany and the United Kingdom (UK), natural gas is more expensive than the cheap coal from the United States, so energy companies in those countries choose to use the cheap coal in their power plants. The pollution from coal is still created, just in a different location, so the damage to Earth's atmosphere is the same.

Going Against Nature

Fracking is being done in several countries around the world, but wherever fracking companies decide to set up, people protest it. These protesters are very concerned that fracking causes damage to the environment. Shale gas reserves can be anywhere in a country, including in beautiful countryside. Critics of fracking do not want to see the landscape covered with ugly extraction sites, tall drilling rigs, huge gas tanks, and ponds or tanks for the wastewater. Some fracking sites have a lot of drilling wells, hundreds of machines working, and a large area of ugly pipework, which can spoil the look of **rural** areas. People who are against fracking also do not want to see the gas pipelines snaking across the countryside to the power plant, or see the land dug up so the gas pipes can be buried.

Many people are concerned about the effect of fracking on the environment.

As well being worried about the appearance of fracking sites, people who are against fracking are even more concerned that it may be causing real damage to the land, wildlife, and nature in general. There are several ways in which the impact fracking has on an area needs to be carefully considered. Because of these issues, in some countries, governments have decided to ban fracking altogether, at least until the process can be improved or proven safe.

Many people think that the structures needed to carry out fracking look ugly and spoil the landscape.

Worries About Water

One of the reasons why people are concerned about fracking is that it uses an enormous amount of water. At least 5 million gallons (19 million l) are used for every well, and in countries where fracking is allowed, there are often thousands of wells at work.

Using Up Precious Water

The high level of water used in fracking is problematic for several reasons. First, people say it does not make sense to use a lot of water for fracking in areas where water is in short supply. In dry regions, such as Texas in the United States or the Karoo (which is a **semidesert** area in South Africa), water is a precious resource. It is needed by the local people and local businesses for their everyday lives. In some places in recent years, changes to the climate caused by global warming have made water even more precious. Long, dry seasons with little rainfall have made water hard to find at some times of the year, and this has made finding a reliable supply of this essential resource very difficult. Critics of fracking do not think that precious water should be used to frack for gas.

The Karoo in South Africa is a very dry place in which only certain animals, such as ostriches, can survive. Despite its lack of water, plans are in process to carry out fracking there.

The Trouble with Transportation

Another reason why critics of fracking are concerned about the amount of water it uses is that all the millions of gallons of water used in fracking have to be transported to the drilling sites in fleets of trucks. This traffic causes harmful gas **emissions** from the trucks' engines, which contribute to global warming and climate change. It also creates **congestion** on the roads. At a time when governments and scientists everywhere are trying to reduce the level of emissions from transportation, does it make sense to use so many trucks in the process of extracting a fossil fuel from the ground?

The energy industry is very aware of these **criticisms** and is working on new technologies to reduce the amount of water that is needed for fracking. In response to people's criticisms, the industry says that we must balance environmental concerns with our increasing need for energy and the need to extract as much of our limited fossil fuel resources as possible while they last.

Hundreds of trucks are needed to deliver the amount of water needed at a fracking site. They cause congestion and pollution.

BIG Issues
At What Price?

The energy companies defend fracking by pointing to people's wishes to keep energy prices as low as possible. The companies say that because they have been able to provide so much shale gas quickly, this has kept down the price of natural gas. The question is, will there be a higher environmental price for us all to pay in the long run because of fracking?

The Pollution Problem

Another concern with fracking is that it causes pollution. Harmful chemicals are added to water to make the fracking fluid. This fluid is pumped underground at high pressure and pollutes the ground. Substances that can be released from the ground during the fracking process also cause pollution.

Dangerous Water

Recovered fracking fluid Is called flowback. It contains not only the harmful chemicals that were added to it, but high levels of salt and minerals that may include the **toxic** elements barium and radium. These substances can leak into underground water sources that supply our drinking water. If that happens, it will cause health problems.

In some areas, wastewater is sent to ordinary water treatment plants. The standards of cleaning there mean not all the harmful chemicals in the water are removed. They are then released into waterways, such as rivers.

The fracking industry insists that fracking is a safe process, and when pollution does occur, it is the result of bad practices by the drilling company. Such bad practices may include a poorly lined well or an old well that has not been properly sealed. Critics argue that even if this pollution is the result of bad practices, it is still happening.

There have been thousands of incidents of fracking-related water pollution in the United States. One fracking well in Bradford County, Pennsylvania, broke down in April 2011. It spewed thousands of gallons of **contaminated** fracking water for more than 12 hours. Researchers from Duke University in North Carolina tested the drinking water at 60 sites throughout Pennsylvania and New York State. They found that near fracking wells, the water contained methane—a gas known to be harmful.

Many people have been alarmed by the thought that **recycled** fracking wastewater could make its way into our drinking water.

In 2016, a report from the United States Environmental Protection Agency (EPA) concluded that fracking can contaminate supplies of drinking water at all stages of the process. The impact is likely to be most severe in areas with already-limited **groundwater** resources. In 2011, the New York State Department of Environmental Conservation (NYSDEC) recommended that fracking be banned in the areas supplying drinking water to New York City and Syracuse.

Following the Rules

To control the amount of pollution from flowback, it is important to have strict **regulations** on the fracking process. Partly in response to environmental regulations, shale gas producers are now working on new, cleaner, and safer ways to recycle fracking water.

BIG Issues
Who to Trust?

In the United States, fracking companies say it is not necessary for them to disclose, or make known, the contents of their fracking fluids because accidents involving fracking water hardly ever happen. However, critics of fracking point to the many recorded incidents of accidental groundwater contamination caused by fracking. They insist that the industry will never be trusted as long as it refuses to disclose the contents of its fracking fluids.

Tremors and Quakes

Another problem with fracking is that it causes tremors **and quakes in the ground. Injecting the fracking water into the ground at such high pressure breaks up the shale rock with great force. Research has shown that this can lead to an increase in seismic activity, or movements deep underground.**

Blasting water under high pressure into underground rock can cause existing **faults** in the rock to shift. This results in tremors that are felt at the surface. The lines on this graph show this movement.

Troubling Tremors

As part of the fracking process, small particles of sand and other solids are forced into the cracks in the shale. Does this cause tremors? Scientists think not, because the huge weight of the ground above the cracks soon forces them to close, returning the rock to its original state. So what causes the tremors? Certainly many areas of the United States not previously prone to earthquakes, such as Oklahoma and Ohio, are now experiencing more seismic activity. One study found that the chance of a damaging earthquake occurring in these regions is now just as likely as it is in quake-prone California. Fracking is believed to be the cause of Oklahoma's strongest recorded quake in 2011, as well as the 180 tremors in Texas between 2008 and 2009. One area of north Texas had nine earthquakes in a 24-hour period in 2015.

Two studies investigating the causes of earthquakes in places such as Texas and Oklahoma suggested that hidden faults beneath the surface may explain the earthquakes. This would explain why other states with fracking, such as Montana, North Dakota, and South Dakota, have not experienced the same levels of shaking. In 2016, the United States Geological Survey (USGS) released a map showing areas of the country with an increased risk of earthquakes because of activities such as fracking.

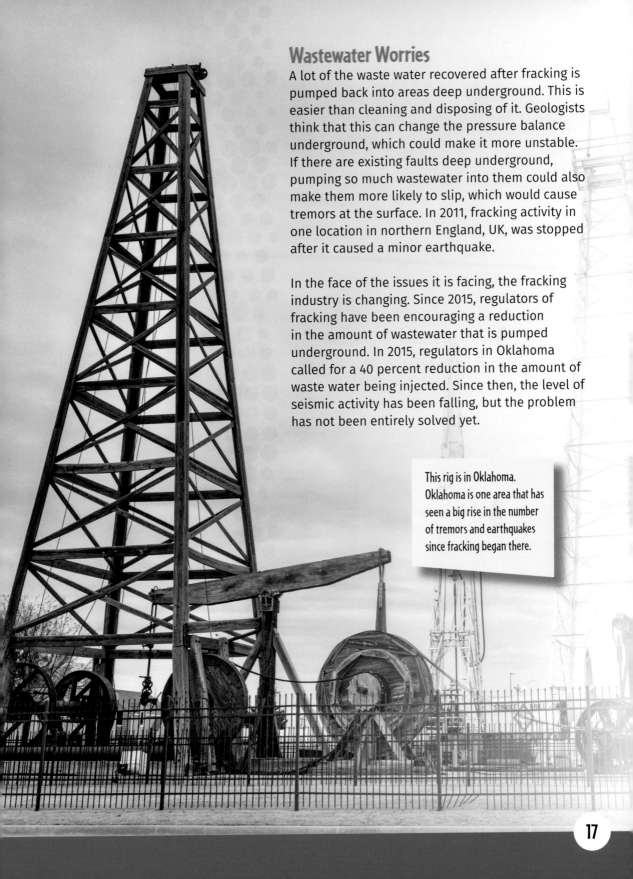

Wastewater Worries

A lot of the waste water recovered after fracking is pumped back into areas deep underground. This is easier than cleaning and disposing of it. Geologists think that this can change the pressure balance underground, which could make it more unstable. If there are existing faults deep underground, pumping so much wastewater into them could also make them more likely to slip, which would cause tremors at the surface. In 2011, fracking activity in one location in northern England, UK, was stopped after it caused a minor earthquake.

In the face of the issues it is facing, the fracking industry is changing. Since 2015, regulators of fracking have been encouraging a reduction in the amount of wastewater that is pumped underground. In 2015, regulators in Oklahoma called for a 40 percent reduction in the amount of waste water being injected. Since then, the level of seismic activity has been falling, but the problem has not been entirely solved yet.

This rig is in Oklahoma. Oklahoma is one area that has seen a big rise in the number of tremors and earthquakes since fracking began there.

CHAPTER 3

Where in the World?

Shale rock that carries natural gas does not exist in all areas of the world. There are large reserves of it in Canada, the United States, parts of South America, and northern Europe. There are also reserves in northern and southern Africa, and in some countries in Asia. Of the countries that have shale gas underground, not many of them are extracting it at the moment. This may be because fracking is too expensive or because there are too many concerns about its impact on the environment.

The Paris Agreement

Countries around the world are working hard to reduce emissions of the harmful gases that cause global warming. Two of the most harmful gases are carbon dioxide and methane. Both are released when we burn fossil fuels, including natural gas. In 2015, 194 countries plus the 28 countries of the European Union (EU), agreed to follow the rules of the Paris Agreement. This is an agreement within the United Nations Framework Convention on Climate Change (UNFCCC). Under the Paris Agreement, each country must plan and regularly report on its efforts to deal with global warming by reducing its level of harmful emissions. Each country sets its own targets, and each target must go beyond previously set targets.

Reducing the emissions of dangerous gases from cars is an aim of all countries that have signed the Paris Agreement.

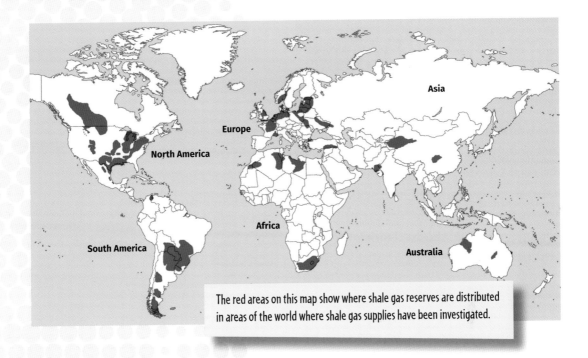

The red areas on this map show where shale gas reserves are distributed in areas of the world where shale gas supplies have been investigated.

With emissions targets to be met, the governments of countries that signed the Paris Agreement are looking for ways to burn less coal and natural gas in power plants. This makes the case for fracking for shale gas less attractive. Although it can release new supplies of gas to a country, it means that a lot more harmful emissions are released. The worries about this have led to a lot of countries turning against fracking.

Arguments in South Africa

In 2017, after a lot of argument, the South African government approved the development of shale gas in the country's Karoo region. However, the gas is likely to be exported rather than used locally. The South African government also has a successful renewable energy program, and some people would prefer that the government focused on that instead of developing a fossil fuel.

Environmentalists argue that rather than frack for gas, it would be better to establish solar or wind power farms in the Karoo, which has very good conditions for these renewable energy sources.

The United States

The United States is the undisputed world leader in fracking. Fracking technology has revolutionized the energy supply in the country over the past two decades. Today, around two-thirds of the country's natural gas is produced by fracking, and there are fracking sites across the country. The biggest producers of shale gas are Texas, Pennsylvania, Oklahoma, Louisiana, and Ohio. In 2017, those states produced about 65 percent of the country's total shale gas.

The Finger Lakes area in New York State lies in a large reserve of natural gas called the Marcellus Formation.

Bringing Benefits

The fracking industry has released huge new sources of natural gas for American **consumers**. It has also created many thousands of jobs in extraction and other related areas. The price of gas has fallen, making it more affordable for people to heat their homes and run their businesses. There is more to come, too. In the United States, around 342 trillion cubic feet (9.7 trillion cubic m) of shale gas that miners know they can extract have been identified. However, the World Shale Assessments report estimates that there is at least 600 trillion cubic feet (17 trillion cubic m) of gas that, although difficult to extract, could be reached as technology improves.

A Risky Business

Although fracking is big business in the United States, it is very expensive to set up a fracking site. This has meant that only well-funded companies have been able to develop this business. Many of them borrowed money from outside **investors** to pay for it, so they have a lot of **debt**. They bought thousands of **leases** from landholders, giving them the right to drill for gas on their land. Then they bought expensive equipment and employed the workers necessary to extract the gas.

The rapid success of the shale gas industry in the United States also created problems. As more and more gas was produced, and the supply seemed endless, the price of gas fell. This meant that the **profits** of the fracking companies also fell. From 2015 to 2016, the amount of gas being produced and the number of companies in the business began to fall. About 200 companies failed, and many people lost their jobs. Some people thought this was the end of the fracking industry in the United States, but that has not been the case. The industry has responded by looking into new technologies and found ways to extract gas in areas that were thought to be almost "empty." Technology is also helping reduce some of the costs of fracking.

The Barnett Shale pipeline in Texas supplies huge amounts of natural gas to consumers in the United States.

BIG Issues
Making Money?

Big outside investors are still investing huge sums of money into the fracking business. This suggests that they are confident their investments will make a profit in the long run. So far, however, many fracking companies still do not make a profit. Some people think it is only a matter of time before investors decide to withdraw their money, which could lead to a crash of the industry.

A Nationwide Solution

The shale gas boom in the United States began in the Barnett Shale region of north-central Texas about 20 years ago. Since then, new areas have opened up to shale, such as Haynesville in east Texas and north Louisiana, Eagle Ford in southern Texas, Woodford in Oklahoma, and the Marcellus and Utica shales in northern Appalachia.

The Marcellus Formation

The Marcellus Formation, which stretches from central New York State into Ohio and south to Virginia, is the most profitable area of fracking in the United States. Geologists think it could be the second-largest natural gas field in the world. Some call it "the Saudi Arabia of natural gas."

The Marcellus Formation has brought welcome jobs to rural areas where people previously struggled to find work. It is also close to areas of high demand for gas along the east coast of the country.

In late 2018, the energy company Energy Transfer completed its new Rover Pipeline.

This shale gas pipeline snakes across a river valley in Texas, where fracking is big business.

Fracking is carried out intensively in the Permian Basin. In the coming years, as production increases, more pipelines and rigs will be seen on the landscape.

It is a 713-mile (1,147 km) pipeline that will carry 3.25 billion cubic feet (92 million cubic m) of gas per day from the Marcellus and Utica shale production areas to markets across the United States, as well as into Canada. To install the pipeline underground, the company used horizontal directional drilling (HDD). This method minimizes disturbance to the surface and environmental impact. A narrow, horizontal hole is drilled first, then enlarged to the size needed to insert a pipeline. The sections of pipeline are joined together, then inserted through the enlarged hole.

Permian Basin

The Permian Basin is one of the oldest gas-producing regions in the United States. It covers about 86,000 square miles (222,740 square km), crossing 52 counties in New Mexico and Texas. The region has been drilled for its resources for many decades, but gas extraction had begun to slow. In recent years, however, the Permian Basin has seen an increase in drilling activity, especially because new technology is helping frackers meet resources that were previously hard to reach. Industry experts think that there is even more gas left underground in this extraordinary region than the entire amount that has been produced so far. Output from the Permian Basin is therefore expected to double by 2023. The building of enough pipelines to cope with this increased output is struggling to keep up, but this is expected to be resolved in the near future.

Fracking in Europe

There is natural gas locked up in shale rock in many locations across Europe. Ten years ago, scientists estimated that there are reserves of 639 trillion cubic feet (18 trillion cubic m) of gas. That compares to 862 trillion cubic feet (24.4 trillion cubic m) in the United States. The geology, or physical structure, of Europe is more complex than in the United States, however. This makes the gas more difficult and up to 3½ times more expensive to extract. There has also been much more opposition to fracking from people in Europe than in the United States. As a result, fracking there is currently very limited.

Southeast France has reserves of shale gas, but fracking is banned in this beautiful landscape and across the whole country.

France and Fracking

France has large reserves of shale gas in the north and the southeast. When companies performed some test drilling here, however, there was a very strong reaction by environmentalist groups. Southeast France is very beautiful, and northern France, around Paris, is where many people live. People in both areas therefore felt the harm from fracking would be too great. The government decided to put the issue to a vote. As a result, in 2011, France became the first country in the world to ban fracking.

In 2017, France passed another law banning all methods of oil and gas extraction in the country. It will be banned in all other areas of the world that are under French control by 2040. President Emmanuel Macron wants France to take the lead as a major world economy and switch from fossil fuels to renewable sources of energy.

Energy in Eastern Europe

Poland in eastern Europe was initially seen as a very good location for shale gas exploration, with an estimated 187 trillion cubic feet (5.3 trillion cubic m) of gas. Countries in the region were eager to develop their own sources of gas for political reasons, too. They depend on imports of gas from their powerful neighbor, Russia, so energy independence was an attractive idea. Several large fracking companies moved into Poland in 2011 but, by 2015, most of them had pulled out again. The companies found that the geology of the country was too complex for fracking. It was a similar story in Romania, where energy giant Chevron pulled out. Bulgaria banned fracking in 2012.

Banned in Germany

Germany also has shale gas reserves. Fracking began as an unregulated industry in 2010, but people were concerned about its impact on drinking water. A five-year halt was therefore called on exploration projects. The big companies that had started work there, such as Exxon Mobil, agreed to wait while the safety of fracking was further investigated. After five years, however, the government made up its mind and, in 2016, fracking was banned.

Poland is another European country in which fracking was largely abandoned. The country stopped fracking in 2015.

Different Views

In Scandinavia, countries such as Norway and Sweden decided that the high cost fracking for their gas reserves made it uneconomical. In southern Europe, in Spain, fracking looked as though it would take off in 2010. But by 2016, all the energy companies involved had pulled out because of opposition from government and the general public. There is one country in Europe, however, where fracking has been explored for its energy potential, and that is England.

For and Against in the UK

In the UK, fracking is banned in Wales and Scotland. In England, fracking has been allowed in some areas. A region called the Bowland Shale, in the northern counties of Lancashire and Yorkshire, has seen the most activity. Fracking tests by Cuadrilla began there in 2011, but were stopped after a minor earthquake occurred.

There have been a number of protests in England in response to the introduction of fracking.

In late 2018, the company was given the go-ahead to restart fracking in an area of Lancashire. The government gave Cuadrilla permission, as long as it obeyed strict safety guidelines. These included that if an earth tremor happened that was more than 0.5 on the scale that measures them, all work on-site would be stopped. By early 2019, work had to be stopped several times because of tremors measuring more than 0.5. Fracking was indefinitely suspended across the UK later that year.

Cuadrilla, the first company to drill for shale gas in the UK, estimates that there are around 200 trillion cubic feet (5.7 trillion cubic m) of gas resources in Lancashire alone, enough to provide gas for the entire UK for many years. It remains to be seen if these resources will be tapped in the future.

Many local people in Lancashire are opposed to fracking in their area.

BIG Issues
What Limit?

Cuadrilla says that the UK government's regulations are too strict. To avoid these small tremors, it is unable to use enough sand in the fracking fluid to release the gas successfully. It has asked the government to urgently review its guidelines and to raise the limit. Critics of fracking, on the other hand, say that if the gas cannot be extracted using these safety regulations, it should not be extracted at all and that drilling should be stopped.

Hitting Targets

The UK signed the Paris Agreement and has targets on reducing its emissions of harmful carbon dioxide that it must meet by law. Burning gas in a power plant produces carbon dioxide. Experts have warned that, without even stricter rules, fracking on a large scale would make it impossible for the UK to meet its carbon targets. It remains to be seen what will happen to the fracking industry in that country.

The Rest of the World

Around the world, all countries are facing similar challenges when it comes to extracting the shale gas that lies beneath their feet. Their geology may make the process technically very complex, expensive, and not economically worthwhile. The possible impact on the environment is creating a lot of opposition among the general public. That makes political parties reluctant to annoy their voters by approving plans to frack. Finally, the pressure to put more effort into renewable energy is moving the story away from fracking.

Big Business in Canada

Fracking has been big business in Canada for decades, and more than 200,000 wells have been drilled, mainly in the western provinces such as Alberta and British Columbia. Today, some provinces have halted fracking, while others see it as providing welcome jobs and other economic benefits. A poll in 2016 found that public opposition to fracking rose from 47 percent to 61 percent over a 30-month period.

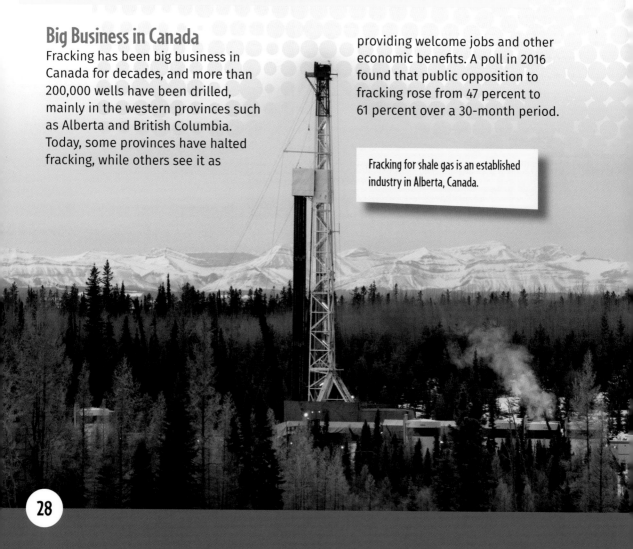

Fracking for shale gas is an established industry in Alberta, Canada.

In Western Australia, there are reserves of shale gas, but there is little support for extracting them.

Latin America

In Latin America there is shale gas in parts of Brazil, Argentina, Mexico, and Paraguay. Argentina's reserves are thought to be even greater than those of the United States. Currently, there are more than 5,000 wells in the region, mostly in Argentina and Mexico. However, there have been some incidents of pollution from fracking, and many people in Latin America are against it. For example, in one 2018 incident, a well burst, spewing toxic sludge and gases for 36 hours before it was contained. The Inter-American Commission on Human Rights (IACHR), concerned with the advancement of fracking in the region, recently called for more information regarding the impacts fracking has caused on local communities.

Opposition in Australia

In Australia, there are reserves of shale gas in the west of the country, but the industry has largely stalled in recent years.

Australia has seen an increase in long periods of very hot weather with no rain and, as a result, water supplies have become scarce in some areas. Five of the country's eight states and territories have temporarily banned fracking. Although the government wants to see the bans dropped, more people support the bans than oppose them.

China's Enormous Reserves

China's shale gas reserves are also vast, perhaps 50 percent higher than in the United States. The country started fracking in 2011 as part of a process of moving away from coal power and to become more independent in its energy supplies. Beijing was the first Chinese city to have all natural gas-fired power plants. However, because the reserves are expensive and technically difficult to extract, this is expected to limit the growth of fracking in China.

CHAPTER 4

New Ideas

The fracking industry is evolving, or changing—and fast. Energy scientists have been working hard to come up with some smart ideas to improve the process of fracking. They are looking for ways to make it easier, cheaper, and cleaner to get shale gas out of the ground, and to deal with worries about the environmental impacts.

Finding the Gas

The exploration of possible sites for fracking is very expensive. Geologists can tell the companies where the shale rock is located, but the detailed structure of the ground can vary enormously between sites. One bright new solution is to use **lasers** to locate the best areas of gas in the shale field. This is done by analyzing changes in the light that bounces back from the underground rock.

Another **innovation** in finding the gas is big data. This means collecting a lot of data, or information, about the conditions at a site and comparing it with data from other shale gas sites to decide where exactly is the right place to start fracking. It can also help frackers decide the different amounts of sand, water, and chemicals to use in the fracking fluid that they inject.

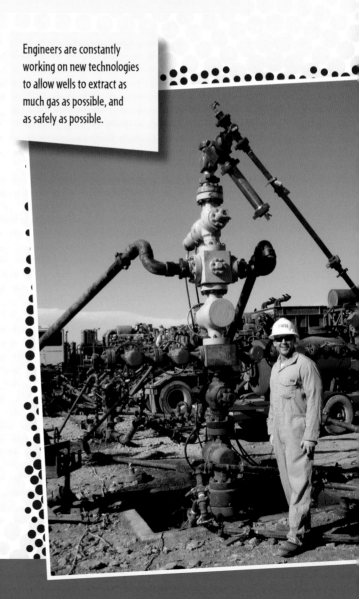

Engineers are constantly working on new technologies to allow wells to extract as much gas as possible, and as safely as possible.

Reusing Old Wells

Fracking today is not all about drilling new wells. Companies are increasingly refracking older wells to access gas that they could not reach with older techniques. One important new method is to use more sand in the slickwater that is pumped into the well. This has two benefits. It reduces the amount of water that is used, resulting in less wastewater to be processed. It also increases the amount of gas that is extracted. Sand is a much greater tool in fracking than drillers had understood it to be. The more sand they pour into the horizontal wells, the more gas comes out. They have also discovered that using finer sand gives better results. The sand particles force open more cracks in the rock, and for a longer time. The amount of sand used per well in the United States has doubled since 2011.

Other smart techniques include using fiber-optic tools with tiny cameras on them to see what is happening as the frack takes place, to figure out ways to make it more effective.

Fracking is a complicated and sometimes dangerous process. Energy experts are constantly looking for innovative ways to reduce the costs and make fracking easier and safer.

BIG Issues
Catch That Gas!

With the cost of fracking being so high, it is very important to make sure that as much as possible of the gas that is released finds its way into the pipe going to the surface. Engineers are finding new ways to seal off alternative pathways for the gas deep down in the well, so that it flows only into the pipe. Different rock formations require different types of machinery for this to work well.

Improved Drilling

Several innovations have been developed to improve the efficiency and performance of the drilling at fracking wells. Better site design, better-quality drills, and more information can all make a difference.

Drilling many wells on a single site is a new and **efficient** way to extract gas. This is known as zipper fracking.

Zipper Fracking

An exciting new technology has been developed by engineers and geologists at Texas Tech University. It involves drilling two wells side by side. One is drilled deeper than the other and parallel to it. The wells are fracked at the same time. The fractures form a zipper pattern, which cracks the rocks more deeply and efficiently than in a single well. This allows both wells to produce more gas. In the Barnett Shale in Texas, the zipper-fracked wells doubled the amount of a typical well. Zipper fracking increases the well's productivity, or amount that can be produced, but it is uncertain if it might make earth tremors more likely. This technology can be taken further, with multiple wells being drilled into shale layers that are stacked like pancakes.

Single Pad Drilling

The idea for another cost-saving innovation came from the offshore oil industry. When drilling wells offshore, it is not possible to build a platform, or pad, for each well. To deal with this, out on the ocean, several wells are drilled from a single pad. Onshore shale drillers quickly picked up that technique for themselves. As shale is a regular layer of rock, companies can drill the wells close to each other. Since the drillers do not have to move the rigs too far between holes, the method saves time and money. The process of taking down and setting up a drill rig can take days and cost hundreds of thousands of dollars.

Better Drills

The drills used for fracking are also being improved. Lasers are proving to be a low-contact way of helping in drilling the wells. Updated lasers can cut into rock at a faster rate than conventional drilling, getting through very hard rock more efficiently. The laser is joined with the mechanical drill bit, and it softens the rock as the mechanical drill clears it away.

Another new technique uses parts called sensors on the drilling machinery. These parts record data about the drill's performance as it drills deep down into the ground. This data can then be compared with data from the drills used at other sites, hopefully showing the experts how their drill's performance could be improved.

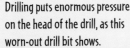
Drilling puts enormous pressure on the head of the drill, as this worn-out drill bit shows.

The Issue of Water

The amount of water needed for fracking costs the drilling companies a lot of money. This is because millions of gallons of water have to be transported to each well. Then, at the end of the process, there is a massive amount of wastewater to be disposed of safely. Innovators have looked at ways to deal with both of these issues.

As these water tanks show, an enormous amount of water is used in fracking. This is one problem that innovators in the industry are working hard to fix.

What to Do with Wastewater?

About half of the fresh water used in fracking is recovered as flowback. The process also creates extra water, which is extremely salty. This wastewater mixture is difficult and expensive to treat, which is why it is typically injected deep underground. Research has shown that injecting the wastewater back into the ground can cause pressure changes that result in tremors. New regulations are getting tougher on injecting wastewater underground, so there is an urgent need for new ways to deal with it. One new idea is to recycle the water that is used.

Recycling Water

The two main ways to clean the water are using chemicals to remove the harmful substances, or pushing the water through a membrane to **filter** them out. Companies are finding that the water does not have to be completely clean to be suitable to use again in the well. In fact, some say that using the water that comes from underground is better, because it does not need to have as many chemicals added to it to be effective in the fracking process. This is because water sourced from beneath the ground works more effectively underground than water sourced at the surface.

In the United States, recycling at fracking sites is patchy, but it is increasing. This is because there are few disposal wells (wells that can safely dispose of their own waste) in the region, and the wastewater must be trucked to Ohio to be injected underground.

Could the moisture stored in clouds be condensed into water and used for fracking?

BIG Issues
Making Water

Another solution to the issue of using precious water resources is a little more far-reaching. This idea takes water from a plentiful source—the sky. Scientists at the University of Texas have suggested using the excess natural gas that is burned off at the fracking site to power a big refrigeration unit. The industrial-scale refrigerator would swallow a lot of air that is humid, or hot and wet, condensing the moisture into water. This is the way air-conditioning systems operate in buildings. This could be a good way to provide water for fracking in hot, humid areas where groundwater is scarce, such as Texas or Mexico. Could it be a future solution to the problem of excessive water extraction, transportation, and disposal in hot, humid places?

LPG Fracking

There is another exciting innovation that could help with the problem of the very high water use of fracking. That is the use of a different substance instead of water. This is liquefied petroleum gas, or LPG.

More Gas

LPG is made mainly of the gases propane and butane. The LPG is compressed until it forms a thick gel. Solids, such as sand and ceramics, called proppant are then added. The amount of proppant can be altered to make the gel thicker or thinner to make sure it reaches to the very end of the well. Once inside the well, the gel flows three times more freely than water. When it reaches the shale layer, it can create cleaner and better fractures than water, which allows more gas to be released. Another advantage is that LPG does not block the pathway of the released gas in the way that water does. This, too, allows more gas to be collected. When pumping stops, the gelled LPG reverts to a gas that can easily be recovered. Compared to water, 60 percent more gas can be recovered with LPG, and 40 percent faster.

Better Cleanup

Another advantage of LPG is that it does not produce dangerous flowback. The waste material can be directed to a pipeline without the release of harmful gases into the air. The waste substances from the ground are not very different from the substances in the LPG, so they do not have to be separated from it first. Using LPG for fracking gets rid of many of the environmental risks of traditional fracking.

With fracking causing so much public concern over its safety, using LPG may be the innovation that is needed to allow people to accept fracking. The gas is transported in trucks like this one.

LPG does not carry poisonous chemicals and radioactive materials back to the surface. This means that there is no threat to local water supplies. When LPG does come back to the surface, it can have other uses, including being used again as recovered LPG. Also, because no harmful waste solutions are pumped back underground, there is no risk of tremors.

Keeping Costs Down

Using LPG can cut the cost of the whole process by removing the need for complex cleanup operations. In particularly sensitive environmental areas, the LPG can even be replaced by other fluids such as **biodiesel**, white mineral oil, or vegetable oil.

At the moment, the only drawbacks with LPG are the cost—propane and butane are more expensive than water. Extra safety arrangements are needed because this method of fracking involves **flammable** gas.

CHAPTER 5

Shale Oil Search

The technology of fracking is not just used to extract natural gas from shale rock. It can also be used to extract crude oil, **which lies between the grains in the rocks. Crude oil in this form is known as tight oil.**

The United States

The fracking process for tight oil is the same as for gas. The sand in the fracking fluid holds open the cracks so the oil can flow out. In the United States, shale oil is being extracted in large quantities from the Permian Basin in west Texas and southeast New Mexico. In 2017, it produced 20 percent of all the United States' crude oil, and experts think there are 5 billion barrels of oil still to be extracted. Here the oil-bearing rock formations are stacked on top of each other like pancakes, so it is possible to draw oil from several zones at one location. Other tight oil locations are the Bakken Formation in North Dakota and Eagle Ford in south Texas.

Shale oil is being extracted by fracking at all these wells in California.

Saskatchewan in Canada has promising areas of oil, but fracking could destroy the region's natural beauty.

Canada—Rich in Oil

Beneath the earth of Canada, there are also enormous oil deposits. The biggest fields are in Alberta, which has the third-largest crude oil reserves in the world, after Venezuela and Saudi Arabia. Energy companies have zoomed in on this area to extract the oil using fracking. As new formations continue to be found, fracking has also spread to Saskatchewan and Manitoba.

Getting Help from Nature

One new energy evolution is being used to extract more shale oil from the rock by stimulating a growth in the number of microbes in the ground. These are tiny **organisms** that make the crude oil flow more freely when they are present. Well operators feed the microbes a high-**nutrient** diet to make them multiply. They break up and attach to particles of oil, allowing it to flow more freely. Another innovation is to channel the fracking water through different pathways by blocking the existing water channels. This makes the oil rise to the surface.

BIG Issues
Does It Pay?

Fracking for shale oil is expensive. The price of oil can be affected by many factors, not just the amount that is available. Political decisions by other oil-producing countries can also affect the price. For example, a few years ago, oil was $100 a barrel. Then the price fell to around $30 a barrel. This meant far less profit for the companies extracting it from shale. They found a way around this problem, however. They kept drilling but stored the oil underground in wells. When the price rose again, they extracted that oil first.

Microwave Fracking

Innovative oil companies are always looking for ways to make their industry more productive and efficient. There is one exciting new technology that is ready to change the business of fracking forever. It is called microwave **fracking.**

Oil shale contains oil that can be extracted using microwave technology.

Drilling for Oil Shale

Microwave fracking appears more environmentally friendly than traditional techniques. It does not use huge quantities of water, removing the problem of wastewater disposal that could possibly contaminate groundwater. Microwave fracking is useful in the extraction not of shale oil, but of oil shale. What's the difference? Oil shale is solid rock that contains oil. It is generally found at a shallower level underground than shale oil.

A Special Way of Drilling

Until now, there have been two main ways to get oil out of oil shale. The first is to crush and heat solid rock, so the oil is liquefied. The second is to inject steam into the rock, with the same result. Neither method works very well, and both spoil the landscape because they involve digging huge pits in the ground. Microwave fracking could be the answer.

A special drill is inserted into the ground where oil shale lies. The drill releases powerful microwaves—roughly the equivalent of 500 household microwave ovens—into the earth. This agitates, or unsettles, the rock, superheating it and turning the liquid water and oil inside it into steam and gases. These move upward through the well to the surface. Once the rock next to the drill has been extracted, the microwaves can reach rock farther away, without the drill having to move. This makes it possible to extract oil from a wider area with just a single well.

Power Hungry

There is a downside to microwave fracking, which is that it uses a lot of electricity. That power has to be **generated** somehow. If the electricity comes from coal-powered plants, that creates a lot of harmful **greenhouse gases**. If it can come from **clean energy** sources, such as solar or wind power, the process does not contribute to pollution. Using a lot of electricity, however, is very expensive, and it remains a challenge for the industry. As a result, the price companies get for their oil needs to be high enough to make fracking worthwhile.

The spectacular-looking rocks along the Green River in Utah contain oil shale.

CHAPTER 6

Fracking Today

People have been drilling into the ground to release the natural resources in it for a long time. But it was not until the energy industry learned how to drill horizontally along seams of shale rock deep underground that fracking was possible. Along with it came the evolution of the energy industry. Over the past 20 years, fracking has transformed the United States from a country needing to import large quantities of oil and gas from overseas, to one with almost total energy independence. However, today, the industry stands at a crossroads.

Getting More Out

The energy boom in the United States has cut the cost of oil and gas for all consumers. As the price has fallen, profits made by the companies extracting these fossil fuels have also fallen. As a result, the companies have been looking for ways to reduce their costs, and this has led to innovation. We have seen how they have pushed the boundaries of drilling technology, drilling several wells from one site and drilling deeper. They have better drills and better information about what lies below ground to maximize the amount of gas or oil they can extract. These innovations are allowing them to revisit old wells, refrack them, and remove even more of their resources.

One of the benefits of fracking has been the reduction of the cost of gas and oil, making it cheaper to power our homes.

People's concerns about the environmental problems surrounding burning fossil fuels have prevented the fracking industry from taking off in many places.

Keeping the Industry in Check

There is no doubt that there are a lot of questions over whether fracking is the best way to extract fuels from the ground. The research shows that it can have harmful effects on the environment, from polluting the roads with trucks carrying water, to leaking contaminated water into groundwater supplies, and causing tremors that damage people's homes. These dangers have led to an increase in the regulations put in place by the authorities. The industry has had to innovate to meet the standards of these regulations, too. Today, wells are designed with casings that should not leak gas or fluid into the surrounding rock. Wastewater is less likely to be pumped back underground—it is removed to another location to be properly cleaned. LPG gel completely removes the need for using water in fracking, and so does the microwave fracking of oil shale.

Fracking Fears

The United States remains, however, one of the few countries in the world to use its frackable oil and gas reserves. Many others have looked at the costs involved and the environmental risks, and decided not to frack. The pressure from communities that are concerned about safety and the global impact of burning more fossil fuels has led to bans in many countries, even those with significant oil and gas reserves.

Evolutions of the Future

Innovative businesses are always looking for ways to develop their technology and their expertise further. Fracking businesses are no different.

Smart Technology

The latest innovations in drilling technology involve both the hardware of the drills themselves and software—developments in data and computing that give the oil companies better information about what lies deep underground. There are even new "smart" drill bits that have computer chips in them to help them seek out the cracks and adjust the drilling accordingly.

Well, Well

When a well is drilled, there is a danger that some of the drilled material will get stuck in the hole, partly blocking it. New parts are being developed to keep this from happening, and to line and seal the wells much more effectively. Once fracking begins, plugs in the well seal off certain areas to make the gas or oil flow productively. These are now being designed to degrade, or break down, naturally underground once they are no longer needed.

Scientists compare data from fracking sites to figure out what lies underground.

Old wells present another challenge. When extraction ended in the past, wells were sealed with several layers of concrete. Over the years, however, the seals have started to break down. This has led to gas and other harmful substances leaking into the surrounding land. The seals need to be replaced about every 20 years, so scientists are looking at new ways to improve the safety of both old and new wells.

The New Game Changer

Microwave fracking reduces the cost of getting the oil from oil shale, and it also extracts supplies of oil that could otherwise not be reached. There is a clear economic benefit for the oil companies, as well as an overall environmental benefit for the communities where microwave fracking takes place. In the United States, the largest oil shale formation in the world is believed to be the Green River formation that lies beneath parts of Colorado, Utah, and Wyoming. Experts think there are about 3 trillion barrels of oil down within the formation. That could supply the oil needs of the United States for more than 100 years, if the current levels of use remain the same. That sounds like a possible game changer for the oil industry, and the start of an energy revolution greater even than the one seen over the past 20 years.

Solar power and wind power are renewable energy sources that do not produce harmful emissions.

BIG Issues
A Dinosaur or a Bridge?

Some say that fracking for fossil fuels such as oil and gas is "dinosaur" technology and should be allowed to die out. Others say that, used wisely, fracking could provide an energy "bridge" between our old dependence on fossil fuels and our development of renewable energy sources such as wind and solar power, which are newer, cleaner ways to power our world.

Glossary

atmosphere the blanket of gases around Earth

bacteria microscopic organisms

biodiesel a form of diesel made from organic material, such as crops

carbon dioxide a gas that gathers in the atmosphere and contributes to global warming

ceramic hardened clay

clean energy energy that does not pollute the environment

climate the regular weather conditions of an area

climate change the changes in climate around the world caused by the gradual increase in the air temperature

congestion traffic back ups

consumers people who buy goods and services

contaminated made dirty and possibly dangerous because of the addition of a substance

criticisms arguments against something; finding faults

crude oil unrefined oil taken straight from the ground

debt money owed

dissolve to break down a solid within a liquid

economies the money systems of countries

efficient able to achieve maximum productivity with minimum wasted effort or expense

emissions something, usually harmful, that is put into the air

environment the natural world

environmentalists people who are concerned about the environment or try to protect it

faults long breaks in a layer of rock

filter to remove solids from a liquid in a similar way to a sieve

flammable easily catches fire

fossil fuels energy sources in the ground such as coal, oil, and gas that are limited in quantity

generated made

global warming the increase in the temperature of Earth's atmosphere, caused by the greenhouse effect

greenhouse gases harmful gases, such as carbon dioxide, that collect in Earth's atmosphere and trap the heat of the sun

groundwater water that is found below the ground, not at the surface

innovation a smart new way of doing something

investors people who put money into starting and growing something such as a business

lasers very powerful beams of light

leases agreements that allow someone to use something, such as an area of land

microwave a short electromagnetic wave. Fracking uses microwaves to break up oil shale to release the oil it contains

minerals substances that occur naturally in the ground

natural resources things we use, such as water and oil, that are found in the natural world

nonrenewable will eventually run out

nutrient the part of food that living organisms need to be healthy

organisms living creatures such as animals or plants

particles tiny pieces of something

pollution harmful substances in the environment

power plants places where energy is created

political related to politics, or systems of running a country

profits money earned above operating costs

radioactive sending out radiation, which can have harmful effects

recycled used again

regulations rules and checks put in place to control something

renewable describes energy created from sources that do not run out, such as light from the sun, wind, water, and the heat within Earth

reserves available supplies

reservoirs large pools of collected gas or water

resources things, such as oil, that are available for use by people

rural related to the countryside

semidesert an area with some desert characteristics, but more rainfall

toxic poisonous

tremors slight earthquakes; shaking

wellhead the uppermost part of a well, found at the surface of a well

wells long shafts that reach into the ground to extract a resource such as gas or oil

Find Out More

Books

Adams, Kenneth. *Oil Drilling and Fracking* (Earth's Environment in Danger). PowerKids Press, 2018.

Dickmann, Nancy. *Fracking: Fracturing Rock to Reach Oil and Gas Underground* (Next Generation Energy). Crabtree Publishing, 2015.

Labrecque, Ellen. *Drilling and Fracking* (21st Century Skills Library: Global Citizens: Environmentalism). Cherry Lake Publishing, 2017.

Websites

Find out more about fracking at:
https://kids.britannica.com/students/article/fracking/609328

For an easy-to-understand guide to fracking with additional links, go to:
http://tiki.oneworld.org/fracking/fracking.html

The Department of Energy Information Administration (EIA) has information on all types of energy. For information on natural gas, log on at:
www.eia.gov/energyexplained/index.php?page=natural_gas_home

Build on a basic understanding of fracking at:
www.livescience.com/34464-what-is-fracking.html

Publisher's note to educators and parents:
All the websites featured above have been carefully reviewed to ensure that they are suitable for students. However, many websites change often, and we cannot guarantee that a site's future contents will continue to meet our high standards of educational value. Please be advised that students should be closely monitored whenever they access the Internet.

Index

About the Author

Robyn Hardyman has written hundreds of children's information books on just about every subject, including science, history, geography, and math. In writing this book she has learned even more about science and discovered that innovation is the key to our future.